CENGAGE Learning

Nonfiction Classics for Students, Volume 1

Staff

Editor: Elizabeth Thomason.

Contributing Editors: Reginald Carlton, Anne Marie Hacht, Michael L. LaBlanc, Ira Mark Milne, Jennifer Smith.

Managing Editor, Literature Content: Dwayne D. Hayes.

Managing Editor, Literature Product: David Galens.

Publisher, Literature Product: Mark Scott.

Content Capture: Joyce Nakamura, *Managing Editor*. Sara Constantakis, *Editor*.

Research: Victoria B. Cariappa, *Research Manager*. Cheryl Warnock, *Research Specialist*. Tamara Nott, Tracie A. Richardson, *Research Associates*. Nicodemus Ford, Sarah Genik, Timothy Lehnerer, Ron Morelli, *Research Assistants*.

Permissions: Maria Franklin, *Permissions Manager.* Shalice Shah-Caldwell, *Permissions Associate.* Jacqueline Jones, *Permissions Assistant.*

Manufacturing: Mary Beth Trimper, *Manager, Composition and Electronic Prepress.* Evi Seoud, *Assistant Manager, Composition Purchasing and Electronic Prepress.* Stacy Melson, *Buyer.*

Imaging and Multimedia Content Team: Barbara Yarrow, *Manager.* Randy Bassett, *Imaging Supervisor.* Robert Duncan, Dan Newell, *Imaging Specialists.* Pamela A. Reed, *Imaging Coordinator.* Leitha Etheridge-Sims, Mary Grimes, David G. Oblender, *Image Catalogers.* Robyn V. Young, *Project Manager.* Dean Dauphinais, *Senior Image Editor.* Kelly A. Quin, *Image Editor.*

Product Design Team: Kenn Zorn, *Product Design Manager.* Pamela A. E. Galbreath, *Senior Art Director.* Michael Logusz, *Graphic Artist.*

Copyright Notice

agency, institution, publication, service, or individual does not imply endorsement of the editors or publisher. Errors brought to the attention of the publisher and verified to the satisfaction of the publisher will be corrected in future editions.

Angela's Ashes

Frank McCourt 1996

Introduction

In *Angela's Ashes*, Frank McCourt tells the story of his impoverished childhood and adolescence in Limerick, Ireland, during the 1930s and 1940s. Written from the point of view of the young boy, it is a long catalogue of deprivation and hardship: the alcoholism of his father, the despair of his mother, the deaths of three of his younger siblings, the grinding poverty and unsanitary living conditions they all had to endure. The story takes place in a highly religious society in which the dogmas of Roman Catholicism are accepted without question. In addition to Catholicism, the people of Limerick exhibit a narrow provincialism, in which Protestants and anyone who comes from the north of Ireland are despised, and an Irish nationalism that is fueled by hatred of the English. And yet the effect of the story, although often poignant and sad, is not depressing. The young narrator describes the events without bitterness, anger, or blame. Poverty and hardship are treated simply as if they are a fact of life, like the weather. And in spite of the hard circumstances, many episodes are hilarious.

The combination of childhood innocence, riotous humor, and descriptions of a degree of poverty beyond anything that contemporary readers in the West could imagine made *Angela's Ashes* a huge commercial success. It is regarded as an outstanding contribution to the growing popularity of the genre of the memoir.

Author Biography

Frank McCourt was born on August 19, 1930, in Brooklyn, New York. He was the first of seven children born to Malachy and Angela McCourt. When he was four, his sister Margaret died. In that same year, the family decided to leave New York and return to their native Ireland. They settled in Limerick in southwest Ireland.

In Limerick during the 1930s, the McCourt family was desperately poor. Malachy McCourt was an alcoholic and was frequently unemployed. McCourt's twin brothers both died of pneumonia, probably due to the unhealthy living conditions. McCourt spent three months in the hospital with typhoid fever when he was ten. In the early 1940s, during World War II, McCourt's father went to England to work in a munitions factory in Coventry, but he never sent any money back to his family. By the age of eleven, McCourt was the family breadwinner. Several years later he quit school and got a job delivering telegrams. He eventually managed to save enough money to leave Ireland for the United States. In 1949, at the age of nineteen, he arrived in New York City and got a job at the Biltmore Hotel. He was eventually fired from the Biltmore and took a series of menial jobs.

McCourt was drafted into the army during the Korean War and served in West Germany. After military service, he attended New York University under the G. I. Bill, where he earned a bachelor's degree in English. He later earned a master's degree in English at Brooklyn College.

For twenty-eight years, beginning in 1959, McCourt taught in schools in New York City. For the last fifteen of those years, he taught English and creative writing at Stuyvesant High School in Manhattan, which was noted for the high quality of its students and where he was known as a popular teacher.

McCourt retired in 1987. In 1994, he began writing a memoir of his life in Ireland, *Angela's Ashes*, which was published in 1996 by Scribner. The book was a huge success and won many awards, including the Pulitzer Prize.

In 1999, McCourt published *'Tis*, a memoir that took up the story of his life where *Angela's Ashes* left off.

McCourt is married to his third wife, Ellen Frey, a publicist whom he married in 1994. They live in New York City.

Chapters 1 and 2

Frank McCourt, the narrator of *Angela's Ashes*, describes his family origins and his early years in Brooklyn. His Irish father fled to America after serving with the Irish Republican Army in their conflict with the British. There he married Angela Sheehan from Limerick. Within a few years, Angela gave birth to five children, one of whom died in infancy. Life is hard in Brooklyn, and relatives arrange for the McCourts to return to Ireland and settle in Limerick. In their one-room dwelling, the entire family sleeps in one flea-infested bed. Frank's father, who is an alcoholic, goes on the dole. Angela accepts charity from the St. Vincent de Paul Society, but her family is miserably poor. Both twins die of pneumonia.

Chapters 3 and 4

The McCourts move to a slum house, and Angela gives birth to another boy, Michael. Frank's father tells him the baby was brought by the Angel on the Seventh Step. Sometimes Frank sits on the seventh step of the staircase in case the angel visits. Malachy gets a job in a cement factory, but on payday he spends all his money in the pub. Frank is washed and scrubbed and dressed in a new suit for his First Communion. Afterwards, Grandma makes him a special breakfast, which, to Grandma's dismay, he vomits up. His day ends with a trip to the cinema.

Chapters 5 and 6

Frank gets into trouble with Grandma when, instead of taking dinner to the lodger, he eats it himself. In a prank, Frank's brother Malachy puts his father's false teeth in his own mouth and cannot get them out, resulting in a trip to the hospital. Frank takes dance lessons but soon skips them in favor of the cinema. He reluctantly joins the Arch Confraternity and becomes an altar boy. At school the masters are bullies. With his friend Paddy Clohessy, Frank visits the home of their classmate Fintan Slattery, after which they steal apples from an orchard and drink milk directly from a cow's udder.

Chapters 7 and 8

Frank earns money by helping Uncle Pat deliver newspapers. He meets Mr. Timoney, an old man with poor eyesight, who pays Frank to read to him. Angela gives birth to another baby boy, Alphie. A classmate offers to let Frank and his friends climb the drainpipe at his house to see his sisters taking their bath. The adventure is a fiasco and they are caught. Frank catches typhoid fever and spends three months in the hospital. He talks to a young girl, Patricia Morgan, who later dies. Frank is punished for talking to her, which is against the hospital rules, by being moved to an empty ward. A cleaner named Seamus befriends him.

Chapters 9 and 10

Frank's father gets a job in a munitions factory in England but sends no money home. Frank has conjunctivitis and spends another month in the hospital. Angela is forced to seek public assistance and is humiliated by the men who dispense it. Then she gets pneumonia, and the boys are sent to live with Aunt Aggie and Uncle Pa. Aggie is cruel to them. When Angela returns from hospital, she is forced to beg for food at the priest's home.

Chapters 11 and 12

Eleven-year-old Frank gets a job helping his neighbor John Hannon deliver coal. His friends envy him, but the coal dust hurts his weak eyes. Frank's father returns for Christmas but brings no money. After his departure, the family is threatened with eviction for nonpayment of rent. They burn some loose wood from one of the walls of the rooms for heat. Frank hacks at one of the beams while his mother is out and the ceiling falls in. They are evicted and go to live with Angela's cousin Laman Griffin.

Chapters 13 and 14

At thirteen, Frank excels in school. His mother wants him to continue his education, but he is turned away from the Christian Brothers school. Laman comes home drunk and punches Frank, bruising his face. Frank goes to stay with his uncle Pat and quits school.

Chapters 15 and 16

Frank works as a telegram boy and meets Theresa Carmody, a girl who is dying of consumption. They make love. Within a short while, Theresa dies and Frank is heartbroken. Frank delivers a telegram to Mr. Harrington, who complains untruthfully to Frank's employers that Frank stole whiskey and food. A priest intervenes to save Frank's job, but Frank decides to quit anyway and takes a job distributing newspapers. He has a second job writing letters for Mrs. Finucane.

Chapters 17 and 18

Uncle Pa takes Frank for his first beer in a pub. He gets drunk and after going home hits his mother. A compassionate priest hears his confession. Frank works all winter at his new job and dreams of immigrating to America. Finally he saves enough money to buy a ticket and sail to New York.

Mr. Benson

Mr. Benson is a master at Leamy's National School. Fierce and short-tempered, he browbeats the boys and hits them with his stick. As Frank puts it, "He roars and spits all over us all day."

Theresa Carmody

Theresa Carmody is a seventeen-year-old girl whom Frank meets when he is delivering telegrams. Theresa has red hair and green eyes; she is dying of consumption. She and Frank make love several times, but she dies within weeks. Frank is heartbroken.

Paddy Clohessy

Paddy Clohessy is Frank's friend when they are seven years old. Paddy has six brothers and one sister, and the family is extremely poor. He goes to school barefoot, dressed in rags. In one incident, he and Frank rob an orchard and drink milk directly from a cow. Later, Paddy moves to England and works in a pub.

Declan Collopy

Declan Collopy is four years older than Frank. According to Frank, "He has lumps on his forehead that look like horns. He has thick ginger eyebrows that meet in the middle and hang over his eyes, and his arms hang down to his kneecaps." Declan is a bully who is in charge of enforcing attendance at the Confraternity that Frank joins.

Peter Dooley

Peter Dooley is known as Quasimodo because he has a hump on his back like the hunchback of Notre Dame. He is five years older than Frank. Frank says of his appearance, "His red hair sticks up in all directions. He has green eyes and one rolls around in his head so much he's constantly tapping his temple to keep it where it's supposed to be." Quasimodo cultivates an English accent and wants to be a newsreader with the BBC. He dies of consumption.

Mrs. Brigid Finucane

Mrs. Finucane employs Frank to write threatening letters to people who owe her money.

Philomena McNamara Flynn

Philomena is a cousin of Frank's mother. She is a large, intimidating woman who helps to arrange for the McCourt family to leave Brooklyn and return to Ireland.

Delia McNamara Fortune

Delia is Philomena Flynn's sister and a cousin of Frank's mother. Like Philomena, she is large, "great breasted and fierce." With her sister, she arranges for the McCourts to return to Ireland.

Grandma

Grandma is Angela's mother and Frank's grandmother. She has "white hair and sour eyes" and is known for her religious devotion. She does her best to help the McCourts but spends much of her time complaining. She dies of pneumonia when Frank is thirteen.

Laman Griffin

Laman Griffin is Angela's cousin. She and her sons go to live at his house after their own is destroyed. Laman is a former officer in the Royal Navy who works as a laborer for the Electricity Supply Board. He spends much time in bed reading and smoking, and he and Angela become lovers. Sometimes he gets drunk, and in one incident he becomes angry with Frank and beats him up.

Bridey Hannon

Bridey Hannon is the McCourts' neighbor. She is unmarried and lives with her mother and father. She smokes a lot and chats with Angela by the fire for long periods.

John Hannon

John Hannon is Bridey Hannon's father. He makes a living from delivering coal, but his legs are diseased, and he has trouble continuing to work. Frank gets a job helping him.

Media Adaptations

- *Angela's Ashes* has been recorded on audiotape, read by McCourt, in abridged (1996) and unabridged (1997) versions published by Simon and Schuster.

- In 1999, *Angela's Ashes* was made into a film, directed by Alan Parker and starring Robert Carlyle and Emily Watson.

Mr. Harrington

Mr. Harrington is an Englishman whose wife has just died. He gets angry with Frank when the boy delivers a telegram, and he tries to get Frank fired from his job.

Aunt Aggie Keating

Aggie is Frank's aunt. She is large and has flaming red hair; she works in a clothing factory. Unable to have children of her own, she is jealous of her sister Angela. When the McCourt boys stay at her house, she is abusive, calling Frank "scabby eyes."

Uncle Pa Keating

Pa Keating is Frank's uncle. His skin is black from shoveling coal into the furnaces at the Limerick Gas Works. He is a veteran of World War I, in which he was a victim of poison gas. He has a fine sense of humor, and Frank finds him amusing.

Alphie McCourt

Alphie McCourt is the youngest of Frank's brothers; he is nine years old when Frank leaves for America.

Angela McCourt

Angela McCourt is Frank's mother. Formerly

Angela Sheehan, she grew up with her three siblings in a Limerick slum. She never knew her father, who deserted the family before she was born. Sent by her family to New York while in her teens, Angela meets Malachy McCourt at a party. When she becomes pregnant, they marry, but it is not a happy partnership. Angela's husband is a feckless drunkard. She loses three of her seven children in infancy, and she has to feed and clothe her family in desperately poor conditions. Throughout these ordeals, Angela shows toughness and an ability to endure the blows of fate, although she frequently complains about her misfortunes.

Eugene McCourt

Eugene McCourt is Frank's younger brother, Oliver's twin. He dies of pneumonia at age two.

Frank McCourt

Frank McCourt, the eldest child of Malachy and Angela McCourt, is the narrator of the story. He is raised in poverty, but this does not diminish his good spirits since he has never known life to be any different. When his twin brothers die in infancy, he is too young to understand what has happened. Attending Leamy's National School, he makes friends easily and gets involved in a number of schoolboy pranks, but he is also mocked by the other boys for his clumsily repaired shoes, which reveal his poverty. The boys make up contemptuous jingles about him. Frank also has health problems;

he catches typhoid fever and nearly dies, and later he develops severe conjunctivitis. Despite these setbacks, he excels at school. On the advice of the headmaster, Frank's mother tries to have Frank enrolled in the Christian Brothers School in order to continue his education, but he is turned down; there are few educational opportunities for a boy from the "lanes," the slum districts of Limerick. Frank is not disappointed because he wants to leave school and earn money. He is immensely proud of himself when he gets some odd jobs and brings home money for his mother. As Frank enters adolescence, he has a first love affair with a dying girl, and he learns more of the tragedies of his world when he sees his mother begging for food and also observes the pitiful condition of some of the people he encounters in his job delivering telegrams. Finally, he saves enough money to fulfill his long-held dream of emigrating to America.

Malachy McCourt

Malachy McCourt is Frank's father. He was born in Ireland and fought with the Irish Republican Army against the British. Then he became a fugitive and made his way to New York, where he married Angela Sheehan. Malachy has a weakness for drink and cannot hold a job for more than a few weeks. When unemployed, Malachy often spends his dole money at the pub, coming home late singing patriotic Irish songs. Malachy is fond of his children, however, and entertains them with colorful stories that he makes up on the spot. He tells them they must be prepared to die for Ireland. Eventually, Malachy departs for England to work in a factory during World War II, but he sends no money back to his family. He returns briefly one Christmas, promising presents for everyone, but when his wife opens the box of chocolates he brings, she finds that he has eaten half of them himself.

Malachy McCourt

Malachy McCourt is Frank's brother, one year younger than Frank. Malachy is the first brother to leave home. He enrolls in the Army School of Music and moves to Dublin. He gives that up and gets various jobs in England: a Catholic boarding school, a gas works, and, finally, the stockroom of a garage. He wants to follow Frank to America.

Margaret McCourt

Margaret McCourt is Frank's sister who dies in infancy in Brooklyn.

Michael McCourt

Michael McCourt is six years younger than his brother Frank. At age six he shows a compassionate nature, bringing home stray dogs and homeless old men.

Oliver McCourt

Oliver McCourt is Frank's youngest brother

and Eugene's twin. He dies of pneumonia at age two.

Mikey Molloy

Mikey Molloy is the son of Peter and Nora Malloy and a friend of Frank's. He has epileptic fits and is known as Malloy the Fit. He is two years older than Frank and is known as "the expert in the lane on Girls' Bodies and Dirty Things in General."

Nora Molloy

Nora Molloy is Peter Molloy's wife and a friend of Frank's mother. She is sometimes so demented with worry over how she is going to feed her family that she is admitted to the lunatic asylum.

Peter Molloy

Peter Molloy is Nora Malloy's husband. He is a champion beer drinker, and he sometimes drinks away his dole money. According to Frank, Peter "doesn't give a fiddler's fart about what the world says."

Mr. O'Dea

Mr. O'Dea is a master at Frank's school. He is especially good at hurting and shaming the boys.

Mr. Thomas O'Halloran

Mr. O'Halloran is the headmaster of Leamy's National School. The boys call him Hoppy because he has a short leg and hops when he walks. He is the hardest master in the school because he makes the boys learn everything by heart.

Mr. O'Neill

Mr. O'Neill is a master at Frank's school. He is called Dotty by the boys because he is small, like a dot. He loves Euclidean geometry and teaches it even when he is not supposed to.

Brendan Quigley

Brendan Quigley is a classmate of Frank's. He is always asking questions, so he's known as Question Quigley.

Quasimodo

See Peter Dooley

Seamus

Seamus is a cleaner at the hospital where Frank recovers from typhoid fever. He befriends Frank and brings him books to read.

Uncle Pat Sheehan

Uncle Pat Sheehan is Frank's uncle. He was dropped on his head when he was a baby and, as a result, is simple-minded. He is also called Ab, short for The Abbot. He is illiterate but makes a living selling newspapers.

Fintan Slattery

Fintan Slattery is a classmate of Frank's. He and his mother are very pious Catholics. He says he wants to be a saint when he grows up.

Mr. Timony

Mr. Timony is an old man with poor eyesight who pays Frank to read to him. He claims to be a Buddhist.

Themes

Poverty

The theme of poverty is pervasive. In Limerick, poverty is accepted as a fact of life; although there is a charitable society and a rudimentary system of public assistance, neither does much to lift the poor out of their misery. For the McCourts, the dole money is never sufficient. When they first settle in Limerick, Malachy receives a mere nineteen shillings a week, for a family of six. "Just enough for all of us to starve on," says Angela. The family often goes hungry.

Not only is food scarce; living conditions are appalling. The McCourts must deal with fleas, rats, flies, and lice. There is only one lavatory for the whole lane of eleven families, and it is directly outside their door. In summer the stench is unbearable. Malnutrition and bad living conditions are probably responsible for the deaths of the twin boys.

The children often have to dress in rags. At Leamy's School, six or seven boys go barefoot. Frank's shoes are falling to pieces, which leads to a comical episode in which his father, after being told by his wife that he is useless, attempts to repair the shoes using on old bicycle tire.

The family's poverty worsens when Frank's

father goes to work in England but fails to send any money home. The children sleep on piles of rags. The downward cycle reaches its lowest point when Angela is forced to beg for food at the door of the priest's house, an incident that makes clear the link between poverty and humiliation.

Alcoholism

Limerick is a town that is damp, not only from the incessant rain; it is also awash in alcohol. The evenings that the men spend at the pub drinking pints of beer—usually referred to as stout or porter—as well as whiskey, are almost like religious rituals. These evenings give the men a chance to enjoy male camaraderie and forget the hardness of their lives (as well as their wives).

The worship of beer is quickly passed from man to boy. When Frank is about six, he accompanies his father to a pub, and his uncle Pa Keating explains to him, "Frankie, this is the pint. This is the staff of life. This is the best thing for nursing mothers and for those who are long weaned." In what amounts to a rite of passage, boys in Limerick are initiated into beer drinking on their sixteenth birthday when their fathers take them to the pub for a pint.

Beer drinking is also a competitive activity in Limerick. Pa Keating boasts that he is the champion pint-drinker. He wins bets by drinking more than anyone else, a feat he accomplishes by making himself vomit in the restroom, which enables him to go back to the bar and drink more beer. His son Mikey longs to emulate him.

The destructive effects of alcohol are apparent in Frank's father, the stereotypical Irish drunk. He ruins his life, and the lives of his family, by his addiction. Another character whose drinking causes suffering for others is Angela's cousin Laman Griffin, who beats Frank up one night in a drunken rage. After his first two pints on his sixteenth birthday, Frank himself argues with his mother and hits her.

Topics for Further Study

- Research the history of Ireland's relations with England. Why do some Irish feel such bitterness toward their larger neighbor? Why has the conflict in Northern Ireland been so difficult to end?

- Discuss the different kinds of relief available for the poor in the Limerick of McCourt's youth. How does that assistance differ from the help that is available to the poor in America today?

- Investigate the topic of alcoholism. What causes it? Is it on the increase? Why do some people who drink alcohol become alcoholics but others do not?

- If you were to write a memoir of your own childhood, how would it resemble or differ from McCourt's memoir?

Catholicism

The people of Limerick are steeped in the rites and dogmas of Roman Catholicism, which they accept without question. These beliefs reach Frank's youthful mind as he listens to grown-up conversation or tries to make sense of what he is told at home or at school. The results are often comical. For example, he looks forward to his First Communion for weeks because the masters at school tell him it will be the happiest day of his life. He thinks that is because after First Communion boys are allowed to go around collecting money from relatives and neighbors, which they can then use to buy sweets and go to the Lyric Cinema.

When the big day arrives, the priest puts the wafer, which according to Catholic dogma is the body of Christ, on Frank's tongue. To Frank's dismay, it sticks: "I had God glued to the roof of my mouth. I could hear the master's voice, Don't let that host touch your teeth for if you bite God in two you'll roast in hell for eternity." However, the crisis passes. "God was good," Frank says. "He melted and I swallowed Him and now, at last, I was a member of the True Church, an official sinner."

When Frank is confused about religion, he simply connects the bits and pieces he has heard until he has something that makes sense to him. When his little brother Eugene dies, he wonders whether he is cold in his coffin in the graveyard, but then he remembers that angels come and open the coffin and take Eugene up to the sky where he joins his other dead siblings and they have plenty of fish and chips and toffee.

As for the adults, they seem content with a narrow faith in which only Catholics are saved. Protestants and others are doomed to hell, and even unbaptized children languish forever in Limbo. "Otherwise," says Frank's grandmother, "you'd have all kinds of babies clamorin' to get into heaven, Protestants an' everything, an' why should they get in after what they did to us for eight hundred years?"

Style

Angela's Ashes is narrated in the first person, and apart from the first part of chapter one, it is told in the present tense. The present tense narration serves the author's purpose well as it conveys the immediacy of the child's experience and avoids giving the impression, as a past tense might, that the story is being told by an adult reflecting on his childhood.

The language used throughout is colloquial and earthy. Slang, Irishisms, and vulgar expressions are used frequently, and these convey the way people really talked in Limerick during the author's childhood. Having a "fine fist," for example, means that a person has good handwriting. To go "beyond the beyonds" is to behave in an outrageous manner.

Some words will be unfamiliar to American ears: "gob" is slang for mouth and "fags" are cigarettes. To call someone an "eejit" is to insult them, and the expression "diddering omadhaun," as used by a schoolmaster to describe a boy, is obviously not a compliment.

The Irish way of expressing themselves is apparent in such statements as "That's a great leg for the dancing you have there, Frankie," a compliment to young Frankie on his dancing ability. Some expressions are saltier. Mrs. O'Connor, the dance teacher, tells Frankie to stop frowning "or you'll have a puss on you like a pound of tripe." Irish pronunciation is reflected in "fillum star" (film star), and occasionally there is a glimpse of what Frankie's father calls Limerick slum-talk, as in Uncle Pat's words, "That's me mug and don't be drinkin' your way oush of ish." The last three words mean "out of it."

In an unusual device, there are not any quotation marks used to mark direct speech anywhere in this book, even when two people are engaged in a conversation. The effect of this is perhaps to subtly remind the reader that everything in the memoir is being filtered through the consciousness of the child narrator. It is always Frank who is reporting the speech, whether direct or indirect.

Tone

The tone of the book is often humorous. It is only rarely angry, even though Frankie might have a lot to be angry about. The humor occurs not only in humorous situations and events but in the way young Frankie strives to understand the world and what happens in it. On one occasion, when he is eleven or twelve, he discovers his parents' marriage certificate and notes that they were married on March 28, 1930. But this mystifies him:

> I was born on the nineteenth of August and Billy Campbell told me

the father and mother have to be married nine months before there's a sign of a child. Here I am born into the world in half the time. That means I must be a miracle and I might grow up to be a saint with people celebrating the feast of St. Francis of Limerick.

Toward the end of the book, as Frank matures, the tone becomes compassionate, as Frank becomes more aware of the suffering of others.

Memoir Genre

The 1990s witnessed a huge growth in the number of personal memoirs, and the genre itself underwent significant change. Traditionally, the memoir was an autobiographical narrative, usually by a prominent person, that focused not on the personal experiences of the author but on the significant people and events he had witnessed or been involved in. In the 1990s, however, personal memoirs came to be written not only by famous people but by unknown ones, too. Many focused on a certain period in a person's life (thus distinguishing them from the more comprehensive scope of the autobiography). Often the memoir was about the growth from childhood or adolescence to young adulthood. Frequently these memoirs detailed an environment in which some deprivation or vice, such as poverty, alcoholism or sexual abuse, played a large part.

One of the most popular memoirs from the early part of the decade was *Darkness Visible* (1992), the account by the writer William Styron of his descent into mental illness. Susanna Kaysen's *Girl Interrupted* (1994) was a bestselling memoir of Kaysen's life in a mental institution. In 1995, Mary Karr published the hugely successful *The Liars' Club,* a memoir of growing up in a dysfunctional

Texas family. In that year, approximately two hundred memoirs were published. Commentators linked the startling growth of the genre to the vogue for confessional television programs and the "tell-itall" nature of popular culture. James Atlas, in his article "The Age of the Literary Memoir Is Now," comments on the openness that characterized the 1990s:

> In an era when 'Oprah' reigns supreme and 12-step programs have been adopted as the new mantra, it's perhaps only natural for literary confession to join the parade. We live in a time when the very notion of privacy, of a zone beyond the reach of public probing, has become an alien concept.

It was in this literary and cultural climate that McCourt began writing *Angela's Ashes* in 1994. The memoir, with its tale of a family ruined by an alcoholic father, anguished by bereavement, and living with the shame of almost unimaginable poverty, fit comfortably into the genre as it was being redefined during the decade. So when *Angela's Ashes* was published two years later, its runaway success was perhaps not surprising.

England, Protestantism, and Ireland

Even a casual reader of *Angela's Ashes* could hardly fail to notice that the Irish of Limerick reserve a special hatred for the English, and they also despise Protestants. The origins of this antipathy go far back in history.

The English first invaded Ireland in the twelfth century, which explains the recurring Irish complaint in the book about "what the English did to us for eight hundred long years."

Compare & Contrast

- **1930s:** Limerick, Ireland, is economically depressed, with pockets of extreme poverty. Unemployment is high.

  Today: Helped by a growth in tourism and high-tech industries, Limerick flourishes. "Combat poverty" groups have been set up, using funds from the European Union.

- **1930s:** A common cause of death in Limerick, and Ireland as a whole, is tuberculosis. Tuberculosis is prevalent because living conditions are unsanitary and malnutrition is rife.

  Today: Advances in medicine have made tuberculosis a curable, rather than a deadly, disease. In 1998, Ireland reported 424 cases of tuberculosis, down from 640 in

1991.

- **1930s:** Although independent, Ireland is a member of the British Commonwealth. Ireland remains neutral when war breaks out between Britain and Germany in 1939 and withdraws from the Commonwealth in 1948.

  Today: Relations between Britain and Ireland are cordial. The two governments work together to secure peace in Northern Ireland. Both countries are members of the European Union.

The Protestants are associated with the English, since it was the Protestant forces of Oliver Cromwell in the seventeenth century, followed by the Protestant army of William of Orange in 1690, that subjugated the Catholic Irish.

After a long struggle, most of Ireland won its independence in 1922. This period of Irish history is associated with the name of Eamon de Valera, the first president of the Irish Free State. In *Angela's Ashes*, Frank's father believes that de Valera is the greatest man in the world.

After 1922, the six predominantly Protestant northern counties of Ireland remained under British rule. This is why in *Angela's Ashes* anyone from the north of Ireland, even a good Catholic and an Irish nationalist like Malachy McCourt, is regarded with suspicion.

Critical Overview

Angela's Ashes was a massive success, becoming one of the most highly acclaimed nonfiction works of the decade. The book won numerous awards, including the National Book Critics Circle Award and the Pulitzer Prize for biography. It was on the *New York Times* bestseller list for over two years.

Almost all reviewers praised the book generously. The vividness with which McCourt evoked his childhood was particularly appreciated, as was the hilarity of much of the book. Writing for the *New York Times,* Michiko Kakutani praised McCourt's skill as a storyteller:

> McCourt … waited more than four decades to tell the story of his childhood, and it's been well worth the wait. With *Angela's Ashes*, he has used the storytelling gifts he inherited from his father to write a book that redeems the pain of his early years with wit and compassion and grace.

Kakutani noted that the book contained little of the resentment or bitterness that a reader might expect to find in the memoirs of a man who had endured almost unimaginable poverty and deprivation in his early years. She also commented favorably on McCourt's descriptive skill:

Writing in prose that's pictorial and tactile, lyrical but streetwise, Mr. McCourt does for the town of Limerick what the young Joyce did for Dublin: he conjures the place for us with such intimacy that we feel we've walked its streets and crawled its pubs.

The verdict of Malcolm Jones Jr., in *Newsweek,* was equally positive: "It is only the best storyteller who can so beguile his readers that he leaves them wanting more when he's done. With *Angela's Ashes*, McCourt proves himself one of the very best."

In *Time,* John Elson described *Angela's Ashes* as a "spunky, bittersweet memoir," noting that in spite of the bleakness of the story, McCourt's humor leaves a deeper impression: "Like an unpredicted glimmer of midwinter sunshine, cheerfulness keeps breaking into this tale of Celtic woe." Elson picked out McCourt's descriptions of his First Communion and his adventures as a post-office messenger as "riotously funny."

Neal Ascheron, in the *New York Review of Books,* called *Angela's Ashes* a "wonderful" memoir and pointed out that the central figure is not the Angela of the title but Frank's father, Malachy, whom Ascheron saw as a poignant, almost tragic figure: "McCourt shows a man who is almost literally dissolving, physically and mentally, in a world which has no time or means to help him."

One of the few dissenting voices in this chorus of praise was that of R. F. Foster, a professor of Irish history, writing in *New Republic.* Although he acknowledged that some of the images and events in the book were "marvelously realized," Foster pointed out what he believed to be obvious flaws:

> [I]t all goes on for too long. ... its author lacks an internal editor, a sense of developing structure. The language is monotonous and the incidents are repetitive. The characterizations are perfunctory: people are identified by formulaic straplines, which are trundled out again and again each time they appear.

Foster also questioned whether all the incidents were as factual as McCourt claimed. He pointed out that when McCourt's father attempts to secure an IRA pension, he has to visit the back streets of a Dublin suburb, but in reality such pensions were administered by a government department.

Foster's skepticism, however, was not shared by readers, who bought the book in huge numbers. *Angela's Ashes* has been translated into nineteen languages and has sold more than four million copies worldwide.

Sources

Ascheron, Neal, "Ceremony of Innocence," in *New York Review of Books,* Vol. XLIV, No. 12, July 17, 1997, pp. 24-26.

Atlas, James, "The Age of the Literary Memoir Is Now," in *New York Times Magazine,* May 12, 1996, pp. 25-27.

Elson, John, "Reliving His Bad Eire Days," in *Time,* Vol. 148, No. 15, September 23, 1996, p. 74.

Foster, R. F., "Tisn't: The Million-dollar Blarney of the McCourts," in *New Republic,* November 1, 1999, p. 29.

Jones, Malcolm, Jr., Review in *Newsweek,* Vol. 128, No. 10, September 2, 1996, pp. 68-69.

Kakutani, Michiko, "Generous Memories of a Poor, Painful Childhood," in *New York Times,* September 17, 1996.

Further Reading

Donoghue, Denis, "Some Day I'll Be in Out of the Rain," in *New York Times Book Review,* September 15, 1996, p. 13.

> In this review of *Angela's Ashes*, Donoghue comments on his own experiences growing up in Ireland, which were similar to McCourt's.

"Fighting Irish," in *National Review,* October 26, 1998, p. 40.

> This editorial describes how the publication of *Angela's Ashes* has contributed to an upsurge in America of interest in all things Irish.

Hughes, Carolyn T., "Looking Forward to the Past: A Profile of Frank McCourt," in *Poet and Writers Magazine,* Vol. 27, No. 5, September—October 1999, pp. 22-29.

> This profile of McCourt describes the genesis of *Angela's Ashes* and McCourt's thoughts on writing and teaching.

Sullivan, Robert, "The Seanachie," in *New York Times Magazine,* September 1, 1996, pp. 24-27.

> A seanachie is a storyteller, and this profile of McCourt emphasizes the wealth of personal stories that

McCourt has at his disposal. He is presented as a man who finds humor in the darkest of places.

9 781375 399609